THE BODY AND
Reverence

written by
D.M. Brock & Tamara Kuykendall

illustrated by
Gary Undercuffler

Level 3
BOOK 2

TOBET THEOLOGY OF THE BODY
EVANGELIZATION TEAM

Dedicated to the Church, including our family and friends,
and especially to Mother Mary and Saint John Paul.

Tremendous thanks to all TOBET members over the years.
Special thanks to Andrea, Kathy, Sarah, Sheryl, and Véronique.

We are grateful for consultation work by the translator of the Theology of the Body,
Dr. Michael Waldstein, as well as Dr. Susan Waldstein and Dr. Danielle M. Peters.

Nihil Obstat: David Uebbing, B.A., M.A.
Censor Librorum

Imprimatur: +Most Reverend Samuel J. Aquila, S.T.L.
Archbishop of Denver
Denver, Colorado, USA
March 28, 2018

Library of Congress information on file. ISBN 978-1-945845-03-1

Cover Design: FigDesign   •   Layout: Emily Gudde   •   Editor: Dayspring Brock   •   Associate Editor: Alexis Mausolf

Excerpts from the English translation of the *Catechism of the Catholic Church*. New York: Catholic Book Publishing Co., 1994.

Based on *Man and Woman He Created Them: A Theology of the Body* translated by Michael Waldstein, Copyright © 2006. Used by permission of Pauline Books & Media, 50 Saint Paul's Ave, Boston, Massachusetts 02130. All rights reserved. www.pauline.org.

All Scripture verses are from the *New American Bible*, Revised Edition (NABRE).

Excerpt from *YOUCAT*. Trans. Michael J. Miller. (San Francisco: Ignatius Press, 2011), www.ignatius.com. Used with permission.

TOBET PRESS

Table of Contents

1 The Key to Reverence   4

- Wonder draws us toward creation; awe keeps us at a respectful distance.
- Wonder and awe are the key to reverence.
- Seeing God's imprint in the world leads to reverence.

2 Reverence for the Body   14

- We show reverence when we see the human body as God's gift and receive it with joy.
- Those who do not show reverence for the bodies of others miss out on friendships.
- Our own bodies deserve reverence, for they bear God's imprint.

3 Reverence vs. Control   28

- Trying to control an experience of wonder can be irreverent.
- Ignoring wonder in the moment is a form of irreverence.
- All of nature deserves reverence.

4 Reverence for the Body of Christ   38

- At Mass, the Church awakens wonder and awe through the five senses.
- We show reverence at Mass in our dress and our behavior.
- If we ask Him, the Holy Spirit can awaken reverence in us.

1 The Key to Reverence

Wonder and Awe

Imagine a beautiful sunset. The brilliant colors fill the sky with light and shadow. Do you feel wonder?

When a mystery attracts you like a magnet, your sense of wonder makes you want to draw nearer.

Now imagine a thunderstorm at night. You feel chills as you duck your head under the covers.

The powerful storm can make you feel small by comparison.

That feeling is called awe, which is a kind of holy fear. Awe does not draw us in closer to a mystery, but, like an invisible force field, it keeps us at a respectful distance.

Wonder and awe often go hand in hand. We might feel wonder when we gaze upon thousands of stars in the night sky. Yet, when we ponder the vastness of the universe, we are filled with awe.

The Action of Reverence

Wonder draws you in; awe keeps you at a respectful distance. What if you came across a baby deer in the forest? You would be drawn toward it in wonder, yet at the same time, you would be afraid of ruining the moment. Awe would hold you back.

Wonder and awe are the key to reverence.

Reverence recognizes that something is worthy of praise and helps us respond to it with love. Though we are never forced to respond this way, we are better when we do so.

Reverence is our choice to give honor and respect when it is due.

God's Imprint

Together, wonder and awe awaken reverence in us. Have you ever seen a snake shed its skin? Or a baby chick hatch from an egg? Have you ever watched a trail of ants, all marching in a row, building a large ant pile? Since snakes, chicks, and ants are made by God, we find them "wonder-ful" and "awe-some." They have His imprint.

An imprint is like a mark or a stamp from an original designer. When we see God's imprint in the world around us, we may sense His presence and choose to be reverent.

"The heavens declare the glory of God; the sky proclaims its builder's craft." *Psalm 19:2*

Man-Made Wonders

Like our Creator, humans can be designers too. God allows us to plan, make, and build things with beauty and excellence, as He does. Humans have composed, written, and designed many remarkable things.

Have you ever felt wonder and awe for something well-made by humans? Maybe you have a favorite toy or game that fills you with wonder.

> **"Conduct yourselves with reverence during the time of your sojourning."**   *1 Pt. 1:17*

God Dwells in Mystery

We are more likely to act reverently when we are open to the mysteries of creation, whether natural or man-made, because they are beautiful or excellent. God's imprint is behind the beauty and the excellence. His imprint is on all of creation, which is worthy of reverence.

Secretly, we sense the Designer behind the design. Even if we are not aware of God's "secret" presence, we give Him glory when we allow ourselves to respond with reverence.

2 Reverence for the Body

Crown of Creation

When God created the world, He saved the best for last. The best of God's design is something that may surprise you: **THE BODY!**

We show reverence for the human body because humans are the crown of creation.

The body is God's gift to us.

Each human body bears God's imprint of love. Reverence is the right response.

Artist:
God

Response to Talent

Think of all the amazing deeds the human body can perform. For instance, when you hear a talented singer who can shatter glass with her voice, or see a young man riding the crest of a giant wave on a surfboard, or watch a gymnast doing a flip on a balance beam, your senses tingle with amazement.

You recognize God's imprint in those talents and find joy in watching such excellence. You are entering through the doorway of reverence.

Reverence for Humans

Even when not performing amazing deeds, the human body deserves reverence.

You respond with reverence when you recognize God's imprint in the people you highly esteem.

Think of some adults you admire. Maybe your teacher is kind and wise, or your coach is inspiring and funny. Perhaps you look up to virtuous saints or brave heroes from history. Do they make you feel wonder and awe?

Reverence Leads to Love

All human bodies deserve reverence. Even if you don't know what makes them special, all humans bear God's imprint.

A boy holding his little brother for the first time shows reverence. He cradles the baby's tiny body and feels wonder. The baby's big eyes and sweet smile draw him in. The boy senses God's imprint in his brother.

He knows the baby is a gift, and he receives his brother with joy. He warms the baby's body in a blanket and calms him with a soft voice.

Through reverence, the boy is learning to love.

Reverence for the Elderly

A granddaughter might not be sure how to show love for her grandpa. It is hard for her to understand him. He has a wrinkled face and gray hair, and he moves very slowly. However, as he tells her stories from his life, her sense of wonder and awe grows.

She realizes how long and interesting his life has been. She asks him questions and wants to know more. She learns to appreciate him as a gift to her. Reverence brings them closer.

Ignoring God's Imprint

Sometimes there are people who do not treat human bodies with reverence. They do not have wonder or awe for others.

What about kids who bully others on the playground? Is it reverent to exclude a classmate from games, or to call names?

These actions are unkind and ignore God's imprint on the human body. Bullies do not honor others as gifts. If you see bullying, it is wise to tell a trusted adult.

People who do not enter through the doorway of reverence miss out on true friendship.

> "Do you not know that your body is a temple of the Holy Spirit within you, whom you have from God, and that you are not your own? Therefore glorify God in your body." *1 Cor. 6:19-20*

Your Body and Reverence

Your own body also deserves reverence.

When you bathe regularly, dress modestly, eat wholesomely, and sleep well, you show respect for your body. Whether you are a boy or a girl, tall or short, skinny or chubby, dark or light skinned, you are a mystery and a gift!

Your body is worth cherishing because it bears God's imprint. You are His unique design.

As your body changes and grows, you can pray this prayer:

"God, help me to accept my body as a gift according to Your loving design. Amen."

3 Reverence vs. Control

The Opposite of Reverence

Reverence is not automatic. Even when we experience wonder or awe, we may lack reverence. We might be tempted to hesitate at its doorway and not enter through it.

Look at the picture of this family at the Grand Canyon. Which person is showing reverence?

We can tell from his body that the boy at the railing is experiencing wonder and awe and is responding reverently. The others in the picture may not realize that their lack of reverence robs them of the experience of beauty.

Forgetting God's Imprint

Now take a look at this picture.

What if the boy at the railing has a different response to the Grand Canyon? Perhaps he feels wonder, but he does not respect God's imprint on the landscape. He wants to make his own imprint on it.

Instead of admiring the Grand Canyon with awe and keeping a respectful distance, he mars the beauty of the scene by trying to control it. This behavior is **irreverent**.

Deaf to Reverence

We are in danger of irreverence when we are never silent or still. God calls us through Creation. Can we hear Him?

Playing on electronic devices all the time is a form of control that leads to irreverence. We miss out on the mystery of life.

When we are always "plugged in," we throw away the key of wonder and awe. We are locked out of reverence. Irreverence separates us from the world and from others.

Praising God means being grateful for your own existence together with all creation. *see YOUCAT 48*

Reverence for Creation

Sadly, irreverence can change wonder into the harmful control of an object or a person.

If a butterfly lands on your shoulder, you might feel wonder. But poking and hurting it just for fun would be controlling, not reverent. Remember, awe keeps you at a respectful distance. Without reverence, your heart can grow cold.

But...

When you see God's imprint on creation, we experience life as a gift. When you choose to be reverent, you are able to find joy in the mystery. Reverence allows you to see the butterfly as a gift from God. With reverence, your heart grows warm.

Reverence for the Earth

God gave us the gift of the natural world—including rocks, plants, bugs, and animals. Reverence makes us want to protect our environment from litter and pollution.

By treating creation with reverence and not trying to control it for selfish purposes, we make the world a happier and more wondrous place.

How to Be Reverent:

- Be open to wonder.
- Look for God's imprint in the people and the things around you.
- When you see His handiwork, allow a respectful distance.

It is good to see God's presence everywhere. You can always be on the lookout for "wonder-ful" and "awe-some" things. The reverence you show will lead to a deeper appreciation of the world around you.

4 Reverence for the Body of Christ

Reverence for God

Reverence prepares us for worship, where we encounter the most beautiful and excellent mystery of all: **GOD!**

Jesus is the God of the universe, the King of Kings, the Lord of our lives.

We are in awe of Him since we are so small by comparison. Yet He draws us to Himself during the Mass through wonder.

Reverence at Mass

In Holy Mass, the Church provides sacred things to awaken wonder and awe. Notice what we experience through the five senses of the body:

TOUCH We feel the Holy Water while making the Sign of the Cross. Both remind us of our baptism.

SIGHT We see the altar which reminds us of the sacrifice of Jesus on Calvary.

SOUND We notice the silent adoration of others in the Church, and we are reminded to focus on God's majesty.

SMELL We smell the incense that rises up to God and know that God accepts our prayers.

TASTE We receive the Body and Blood of Christ, the God of the Universe, into our bodies.

Our five senses lead us to greater participation in the Mass and help us to enter through the doorway of reverence.

Your Body at Mass

Before Mass, you can ponder the fact that you are about to come into the presence of a King. T-shirts and shorts are fine for home, but the mystery of the Body of Christ demands more. Look your best!

Chewing gum or chatting with your friends may be fun outside of church, but reverence helps us to focus on Jesus. Act your best!

At Mass, Christ knocks on the door of your heart. When you open the door, you can present yourself prepared and adorned for Him.

"Behold, I stand at the door and knock. If anyone hears my voice and opens the door, then I will enter his house and dine with him, and he with me." *Rev. 3:20*

Receiving the Eucharist

When Jesus was a child, Mother Mary reverently held Him in her arms. When we receive the Eucharist, we can reverently hold Jesus in our hands and welcome Him into our bodies.

Consuming Jesus' Eucharistic Body within your body is the closest you can be to God in this life on earth!

The Holy Spirit's Gift

The Holy Spirit can open our hearts with a sense of wonder and awe for Jesus' Body.

At Mass, we may be distracted or restless, but if we pray to the Holy Spirit, He can give us the power to respond to Jesus with reverence.

When Mass is over, let your reverence for the Body of Christ stay with you. Bring Christ to your family, friends, and classmates.

Reverence at Mass enriches our reverence for all of God's creation.

"But I can enter your house because of your great love. I can worship in your holy temple because of my reverence for you, Lord." *Ps. 5:8*

Remember, the key to reverence is wonder and awe, which means you can...

- Be open to the mystery of creation
- See God's imprint in every human body
- Have more joy

Reverence is the doorway to love.